Curious Cat's Way Out Bunch books feature
endangered and vulnerable living animals.
The information in each book is gathered
from known facts about them.

Research by Simon Greenaway.

With special thanks to Gray Jolliffe for all his help and encouragement.

© Green Arc Creations Ltd

First published by Green Arc Creations Ltd. 2011

All paper used comes from sustainably managed forests.

I'm Curious Cat on an adventure to see,
What the animal within these pages can be.
So let's read together and have a good look
And we shall find out by the end of this book.

Curious Cat is off to explore Mongolia.
'Help me choose the Mongolian flag,
and I will wear it on my hat.'

Spain

Trinidad and Tobago

Somalia

Cook Islands

Mongolia

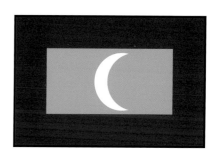

Maldives

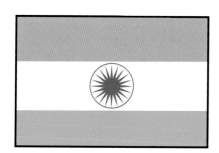

India

Switzerland

Scotland

My oversized ears can hear a pin drop,
But when there's a wind, make it tricky to hop.

Like a small kangaroo I hop and I leap,
But when chased I can trip and land in a heap.

'I wonder what on earth this animal can be?
Do you think it can be one of these?'

Some predators I see
And others I hear,
Small owls may look sweet,
But it's those that I fear.

My furry-tipped tail is incredibly long,
It helps me to balance when hopping along.

'It can sometimes be very hot
where this animal lives.
What clothes would you wear to keep cool?'

I use my pink nose to forage and dig,
Rude friends say it looks like
The snout of a pig!

I sleep in a burrow when the sun's at its height,
But I'll be hopping around in the cool of the night.

'In the Gobi desert where this animal lives
there are many other creatures too.
I wonder if you have spotted some of them.'

Sand beetle

Frog-eyed gecko

Ants

Mongolian Ground-jay

Bactrian camel

Little owl

Sand boa

Earwig

Apollo butterfly

Ants, earwigs and bugs are delicious to munch.
I eat them for breakfast. And dinner. And lunch.

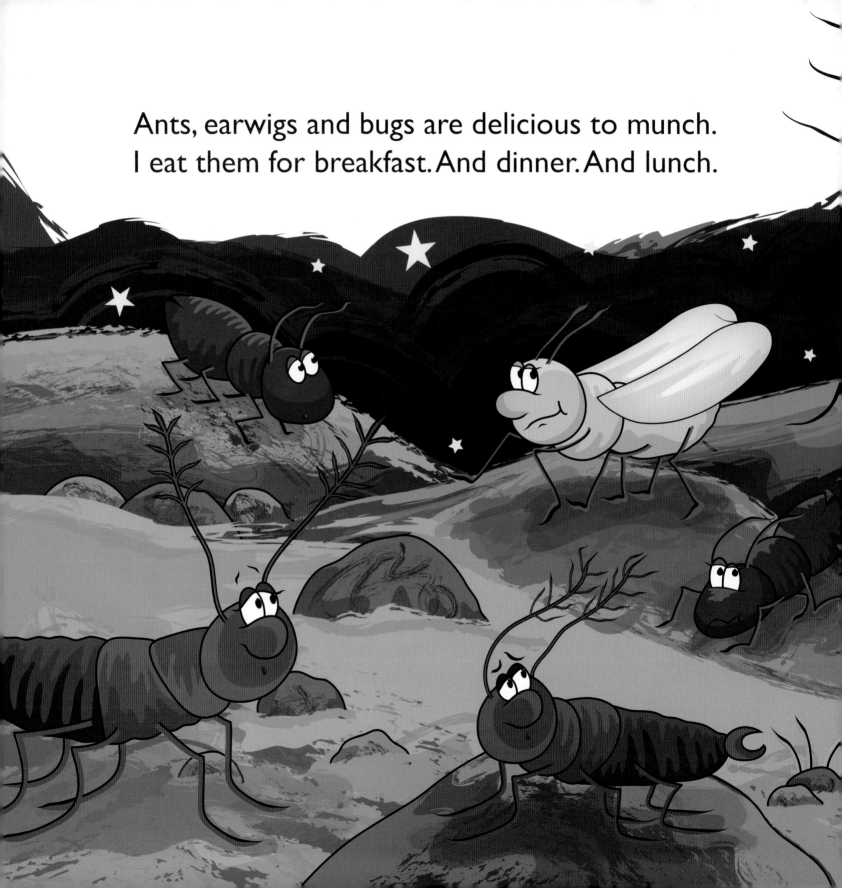

Hmmm. .? A creature that hops like a kangaroo?
What might it be, are you puzzled too?

Not as big as a rabbit nor as small as a flea,
A Long-eared Jerboa - that sounds like me.

Did you know.....

The long-eared jerboa can be distinguished from other jerboas by its enormous ears, which are about a third larger than its head. Your ear is roughly one sixth the size of your head.

It is believed the jerboa avoids going out in windy weather as their ears act like sails and as a result they can get swept off their feet.

A long-eared jerboa builds at least 4 different burrows that they will use at different times of the year.

They have huge back legs a bit like a kangaroo and can leap up to 3 metres in one go to escape predators.

Their tail is twice as long as their body and at the end is a large black and white tuft of hair. It is believed that they use their tail for balance when moving.

When long-eared jerboas are hopping about, they stick their big ears flat on their back to reduce air resistance. Long-eared jerboas are much faster than other jerboas.

They use their jumping ability to catch flying insects.

Unlike most jerboas, long-eared Jerboas are insectivores, meat eaters.

It's not yet properly understood why the population of this animal may be under threat although human activity has increased in the Gobi desert and droughts have occurred recently which may be partly caused by global warming.

If you would like to find out more information on endangered animals and how to help them, visit these websites:

WWF-UK - www.wwf.org.uk
The Edge programme - www.edgeofexistence.org
ARKive, images of life on Earth - www.arkive.org
Photograph: © Jonathan Baillie